D1402879

A Frenzy of Sharks

THE SURPRISING LIFE OF A PERFECT PREDATOR

BY HOWARD HALL

LONDON TOWN PRESS

The London Town *Wild Life* Series
Series Editor
Vicki León

A Frenzy of Sharks
Photographers
Howard and Michele Hall

London Town Press
P.O. Box 585
Montrose, California 91021
www.LondonTownPress.com

Book design by Christy Hale
10 9 8 7 6 5 4 3 2 1

Printed in Singapore

Distributed by Publishers Group West

Publisher's Cataloging-in-Publication Data
Hall, Howard.
A frenzy of sharks : the surprising life of a perfect predator /
Howard Hall ; photographs by Howard and Michele Hall —2nd ed.
p.   cm. — (London Town wild life series)
Originally published: San Luis Obispo, CA : Blake Books, ©1990.
Summary: Explores the physical characteristics, life cycles, and
behavior of various shark species in text and full-color photographs.
Includes bibliographic references and index.
ISBN-10 0-9766134-4-1; ISBN-13 978-0976-61344-2
1. Sharks—Juvenile literature. [1. Sharks.] I. Hall, Michele.
II. Title. III. Series.
QL638.9 H35 2006
597.31—dc22
2006920461

FRONT COVER: A sand tiger shark often swims with its mouth
half open, displaying three rows of deadly sharp fangs. This
husky hunter stalks squid, rockfishes, and smaller sharks.

TITLE PAGE: As big as a humpback whale, the whale shark is a
filter feeder, harmless to human divers—even one who grabs
a free ride on its pectoral fin.

BACK COVER: The whitetip reef shark is abundant around reefs
in the Red Sea and the Pacific Ocean. It sticks close to home,
often in the company of other whitetips. At night it chases
octopuses and crabs, slithering its slim body through openings
in the coral to corner prey.

Contents

The perfect predator

▶ Scalloped hammerhead sharks are a mystery. No one knows why they sometimes gather in great numbers. There are five species of hammerheads. Moving their axe-shaped heads like metal detectors, the bigger ones hunt for small sharks, rays, and bony fishes. Smaller species feed on crabs, clams, and sardines.

One hundred feet below the surface of the Sea of Cortez, as I kneel by a boulder, a shadowy army passes over me. I look up to see a school of 400 hammerhead sharks, their silhouettes like squadrons of bombers against the twilight.

I hold my breath to stop the flow of exhaust bubbles from my scuba gear. I'm afraid they'll see me, but not for the reason you might expect. Like most sharks, these predators hunt fish and squid. They're no more likely to attack and eat me than I'm likely to attack and eat the pine tree in my yard.

If the sharks see me or hear the sound of my bubbles, however, they'll scatter like frightened minnows. I marvel at all the hammerheads in the waters between me and the surface. With their axe-like heads

and their swept-back pectoral fins, they look more like futuristic spacecraft than living creatures.

Finally I exhale, the air bubbles rush skyward, and the sharks bolt. Hundreds of powerful tail fins churn the water, sounding like distant thunder. In the space of a heartbeat, the entire school vanishes.

Many times while diving or filming I've had the luck to see huge schools of hammerhead sharks. These glimpses always fill me with awe and give me more insight into how they live. But questions remain. Why do they form schools? Why do they have eyes on either end of their bizarre axe-shaped heads? Where do they go to mate and have their young?

Those of us who study them still don't know the answers. We've identified more than 400 species of sharks—yet 14 of these species are known from just one specimen each. The most amazing thing about sharks may be how little we know about any of them.

One thing is certain: sharks are ancient. About 400 million years ago, they began to appear in the waters of this blue planet. They swam the seas 200 million years before dinosaurs walked on land; they survived for millions of years after the last dinosaur died. People used to call sharks "primitive" but that's far from true. Evolution has brought this animal to near perfection.

A widespread yet wary fish, the shark may live around a coral reef, in shallow waters, or in open ocean. A few species like the bull shark even travel up freshwater rivers, from the Amazon in South America to the Mississippi in the United States.

Sharks belong to a class called *Chondrichthyes* or cartilaginous fishes. Skates, rays, and an odd group of fishes called chimaeras also belong to this class. What sets them apart? Their skeletons. Sharks, rays, and chimaeras have no bones. Instead, their muscles attach to a framework of tough but flexible gristle called

▶ Coral reefs are rich ecosystems where many kinds of sharks live. The Caribbean reef shark glides up the reef, its yellow eyes ignoring the bright fishes it passes. It's after bigger prey: rays, smaller sharks, and larger fishes.

A nurse shark usually rests in a cave during the day, then patrols the coral reef at night. It uses whisker-like barbels to locate sleeping fishes and crabs. Instead of biting prey, the nurse shark sucks them up like a vacuum cleaner.

cartilage. (Your own nose has cartilage, too.) All other fishes have bony skeletons as we do.

The shark may be a perfect predator but it's not a killing machine. Its fearsome reputation comes from centuries of unjustified human fear and hatred, and the lasting popularity of exciting but often inaccurate books and films like *Jaws*. The truth is that each year on the average, about ten human beings die from shark attacks. In that same period, we humans kill more than 100 million sharks!

Since sharks take years to reach maturity and reproduce slowly, many populations now face extinction and need our protection as much as other species. Sharks have more to offer than ingredients for sharks' fin soup. Their value to science is being explored by a new generation of research biologists, dedicated to solving the mysteries of this wondrous creature.

◄ A sand tiger shark swims near the shipwreck of the *Papoose*, a U-boat sunk during World War II off the coast of North Carolina.

Shark design: much more than jaws

Sharks soar through the ocean like jet airplanes fly through air. Their powerful tail fins provide propulsion. Their pectoral or chest fins act like wings and the shape of their bodies provides lift. Unlike bony fishes, sharks have no swim bladders to neutralize their buoyancy. If they stop swimming, they sink. Only constant forward motion keeps water flowing over the pectoral fins that hold the animal up.

◄ The mako shark is a swift and hungry hunter, swallowing smaller prey whole. For big prey like tuna or swordfish, the mako grabs it with teeth like long daggers. On rare occasions, however, the swordfish saves its own life by spearing the mako! The only marine animals that kill and eat mako sharks are orcas or killer whales.

On most shark species, the top lobe of the tail fin is larger than the bottom one. The top lobe helps push the tail down, letting slow-swimming sharks move through the water in a slightly nose-up position.

The slower a shark's cruising speed, the larger its pectoral fins tend to be. The same body design can be seen on airplanes. A slow-flying glider plane has a slim, sleek fuselage and extremely long wings. The narrow body and long pectoral fins of a blue shark resemble a glider. It spends most of its life gliding slowly through open ocean on its wing-like pectoral fins.

Like jet fighter planes, sharks that swim fast tend to have stout stubby bodies and short fins. Mako sharks are a good example: they have chunky, almost football-shaped bodies, very short pectoral fins, and tails with top and bottom lobes of nearly equal size.

How fast do sharks swim? Figures are hard to come by, since most speedy sharks do poorly in captivity and wild sharks seldom cooperate for time trials in the open ocean.

▲ The shape of sharks often describes their lives. The sleek body of the blue shark, with its long graceful fins, is built for long-distance travel. Blues migrate nearly 2,000 miles yearly, but scientists have found that other species travel even further.

We do know that a shark needs to swim at least 22 miles per hour to be able to jump clear of the water. Several shark species are good jumpers; mako sharks are downright acrobatic! Captive blue sharks have reached 24.5 mph for extended periods. Some may have gotten to 43 mph for short bursts, but not all researchers agree on this finding.

I've spent many hours underwater, watching blues and makos swim in the open ocean. I can't say for certain that the blue shark can reach 43 mph. What I can say from first-hand experience is this: no matter how fast a blue shark swims, it's practically standing still next to the speed of the mako!

Mako sharks often get very aggressive toward blues when they're competing for food. A greedy mako will sometimes chase two or three blues away, darting from one to another as the blue sharks flee at top speed.

Do sharks ever stop swimming? It depends on the species. Some are stay-at-homes. Many bottom-dwelling sharks, such as the whitetip reef shark, spend most of their time resting in caves and crevasses in the coral reef. They keep water flowing over their gills by pumping water in through the mouth and out through their gill openings. Others, like the angel shark, spend most of their time buried in sand waiting for an unsuspecting fish to swim overhead.

▲ The shape of the mako shark, with its chunky body and shorter fins, resembles a jet fighter. Like a jet, it is speedy. When it competes with blue sharks for food, the mako is able to chase two or three of them away at a time.

◄ Angel sharks are flat as pancakes and look more like rays. Their spotted coloration mimics the sandy seafloor and helps them avoid predators. Their disguise also lets angel sharks ambush their own dinners.

But the majority of species swim from the moment of birth until the end of their lives, which could last 20 to 60 years. Mako, great white, and blue sharks rely on constant forward motion through the water to keep oxygen-rich water passing over their gills. If they stop swimming, they stop breathing.

▼ Many sharks spend their lives on the seafloor of shallow lagoons. One is the lemon shark. Named for its yellow-brown coloration, this stocky species often rests motionless on grassy seabeds during the day to keep from being eaten by other sharks. At night it hunts fishes and crunchy critters like shellfish.

Except for the silky shark, all species have skin as rough as sandpaper. A magnifying glass reveals that sharkskin is covered with tiny, tooth-like structures called denticles. Oddly enough, the rough surface of sharkskin greatly reduces water turbulence. Sharkskin is so efficient that it's been studied by the U.S. Navy for reducing drag on nuclear submarines and copied by aeronautical engineers to develop special skins for jet aircraft.

In human beings, teeth grow from the jawbone and should last a lifetime. Not so with a shark. Its teeth come from its skin, not its skeleton, growing from a special membrane called the tooth bed. In many ways, shark teeth look and act like larger skin denticles. They wear away and are replaced by new ones; the lemon shark gets new teeth about every ten days. Some sharks may use and lose 30,000 teeth in their lifetimes!

The shape and number of shark teeth vary, depending on the feeding preferences of each species. Influenced by television and films, most people think all sharks have enormous mouths, filled with terrible, bloody teeth. They think all shark bites are fatal. While working, however, I've been bitten by sharks lots of times.

You'd be surprised at how hard it is to get a shark to bite you. Sometimes I've had to work at it all day. If it's so much trouble, why do it? In fact, why do it even if it's no trouble at all? I'll let you in on a secret: being bitten by a 10-foot-long blue shark is very interesting—even fun. First, however, you have to dress properly. This means putting on a Neptunic anti-shark suit made of stainless steel mesh. Wearing this anti-shark suit is fundamental to having fun while being bitten by sharks.

What does it feel like when a blue shark chews on your steel mesh-protected arm?

Imagine a giant bully squeezing you tightly while he shakes your arm back and forth. The pressure hurts a bit and the shaking can be a little hard on your joints, but the process does no real damage.

The severity of a shark bite depends on its size. I wouldn't want to be bitten by your average 16-foot, 3,000-pound great white. A shark that big could easily break my arms and ribs, and that would take the fun right out of it!

In most sharks, the crushing power of the jaws is secondary to the damage done by the sharpness of the teeth. Once the shark grasps its prey, it immediately shakes its head from side to side. Those razor-sharp teeth slice through flesh and bone like a chainsaw.

Curiously, the mouth on most sharks is located well behind its long nose, so it's hard to see how it manages to bite anything at all. People used to believe that sharks rolled onto their sides to attack. But the truth is more interesting. When a shark bites, it dislocates its jaw, thrusting it forward. Many species can push their jaws clear past their long noses.

This happens as fast as an eyeblink; I first saw it when playing back one of my

◄ Many shark species call the kelp forest home. Others visit it to hunt. Great whites, makos, and blue sharks such as this one can hide among the kelp's leafy fronds and stalks while they seek prey.

▲ Named for the stripes on its sides, the tiger shark often hunts in cloudy water. The tiny pores on its nose measure changes in water pressure and help the tiger shark zero in on its prey. Its strong teeth can easily crack the shells of turtles, one of its prey items.

shark films in slow motion. In many species, such as the blue shark, most of the teeth are concealed behind the gums. When the blue shark attacks, the jaw shoots down and out to the end of its nose, revealing a tangle of sharp teeth. Once the prey is grabbed, the jaw pulls it back and in.

Sharks have other hunting weapons besides teeth. A jet pilot searching for a target uses radar. Closing in on the target, the pilot locates the enemy aircraft visually, then fires a missile that may use heat to guide it to the target. The shark adopts a similar system, using sense organs as elaborate as the instrument panel of a jet fighter to find its prey.

The internal ears of sharks can hear low-frequency sounds produced by a struggling or injured fish more than half a mile away. These sounds occur at very low frequencies, many too low for human hearing. But the shark is tuned specifically to these frequencies.

Shark hearing links up with another sensory organ called the lateral line; it detects small pressure changes in the water. Using both mechanisms, the shark pinpoints its prey.

As it rushes toward the sound of the injured fish, the shark may begin to detect blood in the water. A shark has an amazing sense of smell, able to identify a drop of fish blood in ten million parts of sea water! Even if the fish stops struggling, the shark now has it firmly targeted. The shark uses its nose solely for smell, not for breathing.

Sharks have excellent eyesight. Night hunters like the thresher shark have large eyes; species that hide in sand and hunt by ambush, like angel sharks, have small ones. Some species also have mirror-like plates called tapetum behind their eyes, giving them night vision that's twice as good as a cat's.

▶ Behind the green eyes of the blotchy swell shark is a layer of mirror-like plates called the tapetum. This lets it see better than a cat as it hunts for octopuses and crabs in the dark. By day, the swell shark hides among the rocks and coral it mimics. When alarmed, it fills its stomach with water and swells three times its size.

When the shark closes in on its target and sees its prey, it rushes up and opens its mouth. As its jaw dislocates and lunges forward, the shark covers each eye with a protective membrane. In the final moments of the attack, the shark cannot see but it's far from blind.

This is where that long awkward nose comes in handy. It's covered with tiny sense organs called ampullae of Lorenzini that pick up the small electrical field produced by the muscles of their prey. Using them, the shark zeroes in for the kill. These remarkable hunters can sense incredibly weak electrical fields; in fact, they may be able to detect the earth's own magnetic field. Scientists think it's possible that sharks use these force fields to migrate huge distances across open ocean.

Their sensitivity to electrical fields may also explain why sharks get so disoriented around metallic objects like shark cages, boat hulls, and propellers. The electrical field of metal objects probably disturbs a shark the same way that having a trumpet blown in your ear would disorient you!

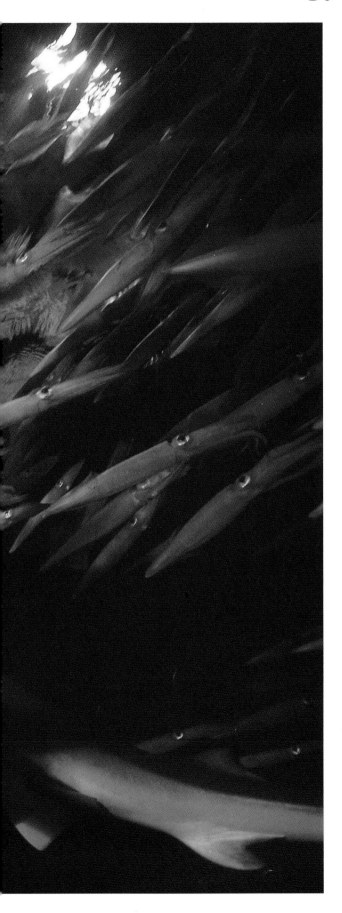

Some people still believe the myths that sharks will eat anything from old shoes to discarded license plates. Unusual items have been found in shark stomachs; however, equally odd things have ended up in the stomachs of human beings. I once read about a man whose hobby was eating his Rolls Royce car, piece by piece! But most people are selective about the things they eat, and so are sharks.

◄ Blue sharks feast on opalescent squid during their reproductive frenzy around Catalina Island each spring. As the small cephalopods mate, the sharks gorge themselves. The squid releases its black ink, hoping to escape, but the blue shark is faster. Those that do escape live long enough only to mate. Then they die, sinking to the ocean floor where they become food for slower, bottom-dwelling angel sharks.

► The pint-sized horn shark hunts at night, using its sharp front teeth to grab prey and its back molars to crack the shells of crabs and sea urchins.

Sharks are meat-eaters and fish is far and away the food most of them prefer.

Mako sharks chase fast-swimming tuna and mackerel, striking quickly to inflict maximum damage. Their long fangs work well to grab prey, then swallow it whole. They also feed on other sharks.

Blue sharks go after octopuses and slower-swimming bony fishes. Sometimes they swim with mouths open, using their gill rakers to strain out small snacks like shrimp and zooplankton from the sea.

Horn sharks live on the ocean floor, their teeth modified into plates for crushing hard-shelled food like crabs, mollusks, and sea urchins. Nurse sharks hunt at night, using a sucking technique to slurp up sleeping fishes, crabs, and octopuses. Whisker-like barbels help them locate prey.

The great hammerhead shark swings its head from side to side to locate and capture large fishes, other sharks, and stingrays. Smaller hammerhead species go after sardines, herring, mollusks, and crabs.

Bull sharks and tiger sharks eat many kinds of prey, including dolphins, fishes, turtles, seals, and seabirds. Tiger sharks also hunt stingrays and even highly poisonous sea snakes.

◄ Like other shark species, the great white wears dark colors on the upper part of its body and white below. This countershading lets the great white "disappear" against its background so it can sneak up on prey such as sea lions.

Great white sharks swim in cold waters and need fatty, high-energy prey like marine mammals. Their robust, triangle-shaped teeth have jagged edges like serrated knives—perfect tools for ripping elephant seals, sea lions, and even whales into chunks. Sometimes they follow whales as they migrate, eating the carcass when a whale dies. Another tactic is a "bite, then wait" strategy; the shark stops after the initial attack and waits for its victim to weaken or die. Once they've fed well, great whites can go weeks without food.

▲ The huge mouth of this basking shark off Santa Barbara looks scary. But this 33-foot-long creature uses its mouth only to filter seawater. It's after the tiniest of prey: microscopic animals called zooplankton. The basking shark gets its name from its habit of swimming near the ocean's surface, as though basking in the sun.

The three largest shark species filter feed on the tiniest of floating prey. With slow majesty, basking sharks, megamouths, and whale sharks strain the water they swim through, taking in millions of planktonic animals and small shrimp called krill. They use gill rakers similar to the bushy fibers of baleen in the mouths of gray whales. A whale shark may cycle up to 1,600 gallons of seawater an hour.

Because sharks are apex predators at the top of the food chain, they exist in much smaller numbers than their prey. Most shark species are widely scattered and do not live in groups. When it's time to find a mate, the average shark has to travel. Its keen sensory organs help in this quest. It's thought that female sharks release chemical substances called pheromones into the sea to attract their mates.

Before mating, the male shark typically chases and bites the female, sometimes violently. For this reason, blue shark females have skin that's three times thicker than the males. Some species like the dogfish male wind their bodies around the female. Others mate side by side. Among lemon sharks, researchers have learned that males are nomadic while females return to the same mating areas each season.

▶ A gentle giant called the whale shark puts up with hitchhikers from human divers to remoras or sucker-fishes. Whale sharks grow as big as houses and may get 50 feet long.

Rather than release lots of eggs and sperm into the sea, as most bony fishes do, fertilization between male and female sharks occurs internally. Shark parents produce small numbers of offspring which enter the world well developed and quite capable of survival. To give them the best chance, many species of female sharks travel to certain nursery areas, year after year.

All shark species reproduce in one of three ways: viviparity, ovoviparity, or oviparity. (These words don't seem so hard when you know that "vivi" means "living," "ovo" means "egg," and "parity" means "birth.")

Viviparity or live birth resembles the way that we reproduce. These sharks develop inside their mother, getting nutrition from

▲ The egg case of the swell shark feels like hard leather and is nicknamed "the mermaid's purse." Inside, it carries nutrition for the swell shark pup.

her through a placenta like the kind found in mammals. Pups are born live, ready to take their place in the ecosystem. This is the way that makos, great whites, blues, and other species of requiem sharks have their young.

Ovoviparity is unusual. The mother shark produces well-developed eggs but doesn't lay them. Instead, the babies hatch inside the mother. After the baby sharks use up the food supply in their yolk sacs, they satisfy their hunger by eating their brothers and sisters. Talk about sibling rivalry!

By the time the mother is ready to give birth, only one shark remains inside her. This baby has already proven itself to be the best prepared to survive in the wild. Sand tiger sharks reproduce this way.

Ovoviparity works for big sharks, too. Tipping the bathroom scales (if it had any) at 40,000 pounds, the whale shark is not only the largest shark in the sea but also the largest fish. In 1995, a pregnant whale shark female was harpooned off Taiwan. Inside her were found about 300 babies in various stages of development, from embryos to live whale shark pups.

The third way sharks reproduce is called oviparity. The female shark lays a small number of large, well-protected eggs. Horn sharks, catsharks, and swell sharks produce new generations this way. The tough sheath or case for the eggs blends with seaweeds growing on the ocean floor. Inside is a very large yolk sac, where the baby shark grows before hatching some ten months later.

When it's time to be born, the swell shark pup leaves its sturdy home. Using hook-like scales along its back, it inches forward and out. The 6-inch-long pup can now begin to hunt crabs, blacksmith fishes, and other prey.

These days, we're finding out more about the learning abilities of sharks, whose brain to body ratio is larger than those of bony fishes. In longterm experiments on vision and other senses, sharks have been taught to carry out simple tasks as well as birds do.

Another area of research involves territory defense. Although many sharks roam freely about the ocean, certain species defend their home turf. Gray reef sharks and blacknose sharks patrol their territories and use body language, such as arching their backs and grinding their teeth, to warn off intruders.

We're also learning more migration secrets. Whale sharks and basking sharks travel far, searching for plankton. Lemon sharks migrate to mate at certain lagoons each year. The larger hammerheads seasonally migrate in groups and at mating time. Satellite tracking devices have even documented a great white making a speedy swim from Africa to Australia—and back.

Sharks also cooperate to hunt, we've found. Groups of thresher sharks round up squid or fishes, then stun or kill the prey using their tails, which are as long as their bodies. Blue sharks sometimes feed together

▼ To learn more about sharks in the wild, human researchers examine and tag the animals. Since many lemon sharks live in the shallow waters off Florida, they are often studied by biologists.

► Open ocean is home to many shark species, including the sand tiger. It begins hunting even before birth by eating its siblings. The hungry sand tiger preys on bony fishes. Sometimes, however, this shark "protects" smaller fishes by letting them swim near it.

▲ The stripes on a tiger shark often fade as it grows older. The teeth of this predator are shaped like the blades of a sickle.

during the mass spawning of squid. Pack hunting has now been documented among species big and small, including lantern-sharks, copper sharks, and spiny dogfish.

What about the feeding frenzy associated with sharks? It's no myth. Sharks can get very excited when confronted with too much prey, such as a large school of tasty fishes. They'll begin attacking the fish in a rapid, crazy way, and end by attacking each other on occasion. Tuna, marlin, and other large fishes have feeding frenzies, too.

Studies are also being done on mutualism, the helping behaviors between sharks and other species. Suckerfishes called remoras attach themselves like Velcro to sharks; we used to think they were just hitching free rides. Recently we've learned that remoras often earn their keep by ridding sharks of skin parasites.

I've also had the good fortune to see hammerhead sharks and other species visit "cleaning stations," where mutual trust lets predator and prey meet. Instead of eating an angelfish, the shark will let it clean its gill slits and mouth. In this way, the hammerhead gets rid of troublesome parasites, and the cleaner fish gets a free meal. Butterflyfishes, shrimp, and other species also run cleaning stations.

▼ Blue sharks sometimes cooperate with other species, feeding next to barracuda and seabirds on huge schools of anchovies. Blues also eat a wide variety of prey, from herring to flying fish to hake.

◄Chimaeras or ratfish belong to the same order as sharks but look very different. Most live at great depths in the ocean. This is the spotted ratfish, sometimes found in shallower waters.

The least shark-like critter in the family may be the wobbegong of the South Pacific. Flat, frilly, and polka-dotted to resemble rocks or sand, the wobbegong sits tight, waiting to pounce on crabs, fishes, or mollusks. Unsuspecting divers sometimes step on them and get a nasty bite.

Another unusual species is the cookiecutter shark. Its cute name might make you think it's harmless, but this 20-inch carnivore can chomp cookie-sized holes out of much larger prey, from seals and fishes to whales. When the bold cookiecutter approaches a tasty-looking victim, it clamps its mouth onto it, then bites and runs. The prey survives, minus a round plug of its flesh.

In the same class as sharks are their close relatives, rays and skates. Most of the 540 species have flat bodies with eyes on the topside, gill slits and mouth on the bottom. Some wear skins that match their surroundings and use ambush to hunt prey. Many have long tails with potent stingers. Five species come equipped with pectoral fins that give potential attackers a severe electric shock. Other rays hunt by swimming or filter feeding. The highly endangered sawfish has a long beak lined with 30 pairs of teeth to hunt and to defend itself.

◄The wobbegong, a carpetshark found off Australia and South Pacific islands, looks like a spotted blob with fringes. Its skin is a perfect copy of its rocky, sandy environment. Some wobbegongs leave the sea briefly to climb from one tidepool to another.

Rays get as big as the two-ton manta ray that soars as gracefully as a bird through the seas. As a diver, I've often experienced the fearless and friendly behavior of this intelligent beast as it filter feeds on plankton, using two lobes on its head to steer food toward its mouth. I've also gotten to witness the courtship of bat rays. Hundreds at a time, they do a slow circling dance in the water before mating. It's an unforgettable sight.

Although related to sharks, chimaeras, also called ratfishes, look quite different. Most have long tapering bodies, ending in a whiplike tail. Huge eyes capture the feeble light at the depths where they live. Their teeth are fused into plates to crush shellfish they find buried in the silt. Male chimaeras have a tooth-like structure on their foreheads that may serve a purpose during courtship; so far, no one except another chimaera has ever gotten to see their mating rituals.

▼ Manta rays are huge and gentle. They filter feed on tiny sea animals called zooplankton. Lucky divers sometimes hitch a ride on a manta. Here the diver holds onto a pair of remora fishes that have attached themselves to the ray. Also called suckerfishes, remoras often eat skin parasites that trouble the ray

► In Australian waters, human divers collecting abalone often feel safer inside a steel cage. Great white sharks in these warm shallow seas go after big prey and might mistake a human being for their preferred food.

▼ Angel sharks love to munch a bunch of squid—especially ones that aren't moving. Each spring, after millions of squid mate and lay eggs, they die. As the soft bodies of dead squid pile up, angel sharks stuff themselves. Once the angel sharks are full, they don't bother to eat squid eggs. That's one of nature's nifty ways to allow a new generation to survive.

Taken as a group, sharks tend to be harmless and small. Most are under three feet long. The pygmy shark could fit in your hand. Even mammoth species like whale sharks won't hurt you. The majority of species live far from human activity: in deep waters, around coral reefs or on the sea bottom. Unlike the ravenous monster in *Jaws*, most sharks hunt and eat less than other fishes and mammals.

But people fear what they don't understand. You've probably never seen a wild shark with your own eyes. You've been fed a thrilling but cruelly wrong image by Hollywood and books—and that's all you know.

Don't get me wrong, dangerous sharks do exist; some 25 species have attacked human beings. About 70% of all attacks have come from seven species, mainly the great white and the tiger sharks.

Does that mean that we should exterminate those seven species to make the oceans safer? No! Because even these fierce sharks almost never bite human beings. Almost never.

Those of us who dive for a living have seen

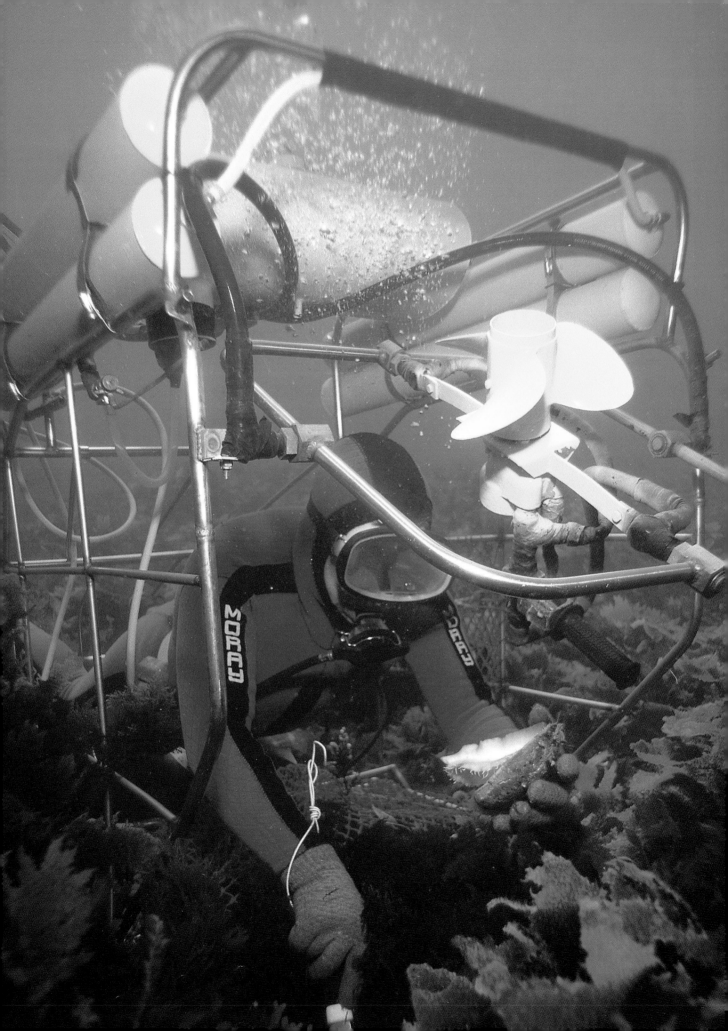

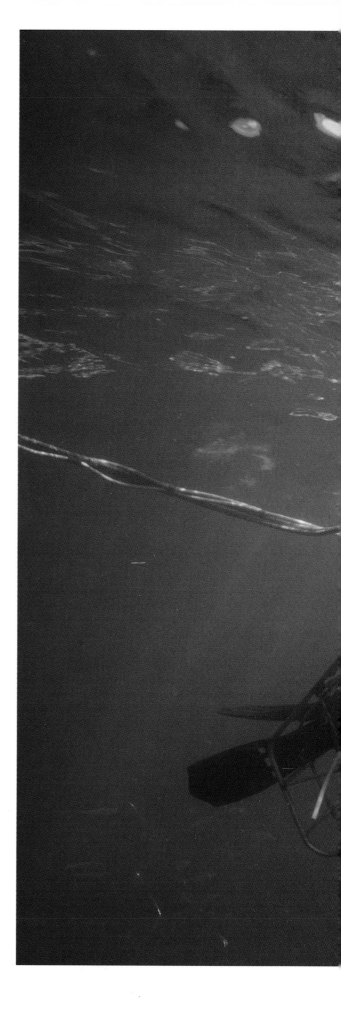

► In order to take photographs, this great white shark has been attracted to the cage with the human diver in it, using fishes and fish blood as bait. If the diver were unprotected, he could be in danger. The great white could mistake him for prey. Scientists have discovered that metal cages have electrical fields that greatly disturb the sense organs of sharks.

thousands of wild sharks, and we've gotten to know how rare "almost never" is. Around the world each year, about 100 people suffer shark attacks; on the average, fewer than ten attacks are fatal. These numbers have remained nearly the same for decades, even though each year, more millions of people swim, surf, and dive in the ocean.

White sharks like fat-rich prey, such as seals. They're no more likely to eat a human being than you are to eat a wristwatch. Most attacks happen in murky water, when a great white mistakes a surfer or boogie boarder for something it normally eats.

These attacks are more like "tastes" than "bites." If a one-ton shark really wanted you for dinner, you'd probably be a goner. Because a shark's teeth are huge and sharp, its attack often causes injuries even when the shark realizes its mistake and leaves.

Experienced divers know this, and diving with sharks is something we enjoy. To do underwater photography, we often use fish baits to attract sharks within camera range. (Some of the photos in this book could not have been taken otherwise.) The blood and

noise produced by speared fishes can bring sharks close in; often, however, it doesn't. One year, I spent a month diving in the South Pacific and never got close enough for one good photo. Sharks generally fear

▼ Global warming and the loss of coral reefs affects sharks, too. Many sharks live and hunt in this rich environment. Without them as top predators, reefs may change in ways we can't predict.

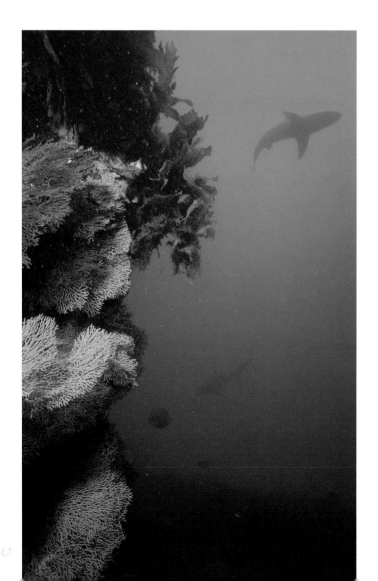

divers much more than divers fear sharks, for good reason.

There is another large predator on this planet that makes the shark look tame. This creature has wiped out hundreds of animal species, pushing more into extinction each day, including entire populations of sharks. This creature is the most terrible creature-eater of all: man.

Human beings kill over 100 million sharks each year. Only half that number are eaten. Many are killed by fishermen while catching tuna or swordfish, a wasteful practice called bycatch. For example, nearly two million blue sharks, once plentiful off the coast of southern California, die in gillnets or drift nets each year. In the Gulf of Mexico, oceanic whitetip and silky shark numbers have fallen dramatically for the same reason.

Finning is the cruel practice of collecting shark's fins for use in soup and folk remedies. After slicing the fins off a living shark, fishermen return the maimed animal to the sea. Unable to hunt or swim, the shark slowly dies. The market in Asia for shark's fins is huge and profitable. They're a prestige food and can bring over $200 a pound. The soupfin shark and dozens of other species, from the whale shark to the blacktip, are hunted for their fins.

A shameful number are killed for sport, for trophies like shark jaws, or as pests. Around the British Isles, the harmless basking shark was nearly wiped out by spear-hunting with explosives. Sports fishermen have long targeted female sharks, since they make bigger trophies. Because they often carry future generations, many die when one female shark is caught.

Ocean pollution, from plastic debris to oil, also harms sharks. As top predators, sharks absorb large amounts of mercury and other toxins from the prey they eat. Shark offspring are extra vulnerable, since females tend to have nurseries near the shore where pollution is highest.

Habitat loss, especially the decline of coral reefs and kelp forests, removes hunting and breeding areas for sharks.

Sharks also have natural enemies in the wild, from orcas to other sharks. For these reasons and more, many shark populations are in deep trouble: the list of endangered or threatened sharks has more than 60 species on it, including basking sharks, blues, lemon sharks, threshers, spiny dogfish, soupfin sharks, and porbeagles.

Although ignorance still causes many people to fear and hate sharks, they do have human allies. The United States and other countries have passed laws to protect certain species and ban finning. Groups from the Cousteau Society to Defenders of Wildlife work hard to conserve shark species and promote ecotourism activities, like photography safaris and shark watching. Organizations like Bite-Back urge retailers and consumers to stop serving sharks on menus and selling shark products in stores.

Scientists value sharks for many reasons. Shark eye lenses are now used for human cornea transplants; an extract from their cartilage grows skin grafts for burn victims. These ancient animals have amazing immune systems and are almost disease-free; when researchers understand how they do it, the knowledge may save human lives.

Some people say: who cares if we kill off

▲ The Caribbean reef shark is a photographer favorite. Once abundant, it too has been fished out in some areas. Because sharks reproduce slowly, human activities are threatening their populations everywhere.

all the sharks? Who will miss them? I will! Millions of sports divers, surfers, marine enthusiasts, and photographers will! People everywhere, young and old, who feel the wilderness slipping away, who see the disappearance of rhinos, tigers, and all the creatures that make the wilderness wild: they will miss sharks, too.

What a tragedy this would be, to exterminate one of the world's most ancient, successful, and interesting creatures. But this doesn't have to happen. All it takes is for you to learn the truth about sharks and take action, from telling others to doing volunteer work with a scientist. The ocean is our last great wilderness; saving it and the sharks in it is up to us. Will you help?

Secrets of sharks

- Sharks wear out their teeth quickly. New teeth soon grow in to replace old ones, though. Some sharks may use and lose 30,000 teeth during their lives!

- A silky shark is the only species with smooth hide instead of sandpapery skin.

- Shark babies are called pups. A scalloped hammerhead female has 15 to 30 pups at a time. The bull shark gives birth to one to 13 live young

- The world's largest fish, the whale shark, can grow 50 feet long—bigger than a humpback whale.

- Huge basking sharks live on ocean "soup." As they swim, they strain seawater through their bristly gill rakers to feed on tiny animals called zooplankton.

- The great white shark, a superpredator, keeps an eye on things by holding its head out of water.

- The thresher shark has a tail as long as its 5-foot body; it uses its heavy tail to round up fishes, then clobber its prey.

- Many species of rays swim together in large groups, using their wing-like fins to move and to leap out of the sea.

- In the movies, the sight of a shark's big dorsal fin is always bad news. But in real life, sometimes the dorsal fin belongs to a dolphin or a basking shark, a huge but harmless species that often swims near the surface.

- Sharks are fast-swimming nomads of the sea. Scientists tagged a great white shark that migrated from Africa to Australia and back, a round-trip journey of 12,400 miles, in nine months.

◄ Unique among sharks, the great white is able to see well above water also. It sometimes circles boats and stares at the occupants with its cold black eyes. The nose of the great white shark can smell blood in the water from a long distance away.

Glossary

Ampullae of Lorenzini. Hundreds of tiny pores on a shark's head that connect to jelly-filled sacs inside. Using them, a shark can detect the electrical field given off by a small fish or one that's hidden in the sand.

Apex predator. A hunter at the top or apex of its food web, such as a shark in the sea or a lion on land.

Barbels. Slim feeler organs near the nostrils or jaws of some bottom-dwelling shark species. They act like cat's whiskers, helping the shark sense its prey.

Bycatch. Unwanted fish, often sharks or rays, caught in nets or other fishing gear and thrown away by fishermen. Millions of sharks die this way each year.

Cartilage. Tough, flexible gristle that makes up the skeleton of a shark instead of bone. Human beings also have cartilage in their ears and noses.

Cartilaginous. Fishes without a bony skeleton, such as sharks, rays, and skates.

Countershading. Camouflage used by predators like sharks. Their bodies are dark above and light-colored below, helping to hide them from the prey they hunt.

Denticles. Scale-like structures resembling small sharp teeth that cover the skin of sharks. The actual teeth of a shark look like large denticles; they grow from a tooth bed and are replaced often.

Filter feed. A feeding strategy used by some sharks and rays, such as the basking shark and the manta ray. Filter feeders strain microscopic animals called zooplankton from the water, using comb-like gill rakers.

Finning. The gruesome practice of catching a wild shark and removing its fins, then throwing the maimed animal back into the sea. Unable to hunt or swim, it will slowly die.

Gill rakers. A series of sticky, bristly, comb-like structures found in the throats of filter feeding species, such as the basking shark. Like the baleen in a gray whale's mouth, gill rakers strain huge amounts of seawater to capture millions of zooplankton.

Lateral line. A sensory organ found along the sides of sharks and other fishes. Inside the shark, fluid in a system of tiny canals detects the vibrations and sound waves of the shark's prey, which helps the animal zero in for the attack.

Pheromone. A chemical substance released by some shark species; it's thought that female sharks use it to let male sharks know they are ready to mate. Other species, from flying moths to mammals, use pheromones, too.

Oviparity. Egg-laying, one of three ways in which sharks reproduce. Protected by a leathery case, eggs are hidden by the mother. Months later the young hatch, now able to fend for themselves. Horn sharks use this method.

Ovoviviparity. Another way in which sharks reproduce. The mother develops eggs but doesn't lay them; instead, the babies hatch inside her. After they use up the food supply in their yolk sacs, the babies may eat one another until only one or two is left to be born. Sand tiger sharks reproduce this way.

Scuba. An acronym that stands for Self-Contained Underwater Breathing Apparatus. Although Captain Jacques Cousteau did not invent the first underwater breathing device, his scuba gear made diving practical and popular.

Tapetum. A layer of mirror-like plates or cells behind the retina of a shark's eye that lets it see very well in low light. Cats and other creatures get their excellent night vision this way.

Viviparity. Giving birth to fully formed live young, the method used by blue sharks and other species to reproduce. The young develop inside the mother and are nourished by her through a placenta, like mammals.

Zooplankton. Free-floating microscopic animals found in large numbers in the sea. Like the tiny shrimp called krill, they are a key food source for filter feeders such as the whale shark and the megamouth, as well as for marine mammals like blue whales.

◄ Underwater wildlife photography is hard work—just ask Howard and Michele Hall. For the IMAX® films, they use a special camera and lights like these. To photograph the footage for the film, Howard drags the 1,200-pound IMAX® camera along the seafloor.

Where to see sharks

In the wild: diving trips to see and film sharks are available from a number of tour companies to a variety of locales, including: southern California, southern Australia, Florida, Hawaii, the Bahamas, and Mexico's Sea of Cortez. In Asia and elsewhere, tour companies offer boat trips to see the seasonal gathering of basking sharks.

In captivity: over 100 aquaria & zoos worldwide offer education on saving sharks and have species on display, often in realistic reef or ocean settings. Aquarium holdings change over time; call or check online first before visiting.

- **USA:** Scripps Aquarium (San Diego), Long Beach Aquarium, Monterey Bay Aquarium (Monterey), Steinhardt Aquarium (San Francisco) CA; Ocean Journey Aquarium, Denver CO; Mystic Aquarium, CT; Florida Aquarium (Tampa), Gulfarium (Ft Walton Beach), Living Seas at EPCOT Center FL; Georgia Aquarium, Atlanta GA; Waikiki Aquarium, Honolulu HI; Shedd Aquarium, Chicago IL; Newport Aquarium, KY; Aquarium of the Americas, New Orleans LA; National Aquarium in Baltimore MD; New York Aquarium (Coney Island), Long Island Aquarium NY; Oregon Coast Aquarium OR; South Carolina Aquarium, Charleston SC; Tennessee Aquarium, Chattanooga TN; Moody Gardens Aquarium Pyramid (Galveston Island), Dallas Zoo (Dallas), Ft. Worth Zoo & Aquarium (Ft Worth), Downtown Aquarium, (Houston) TX; Pt Defiance Zoo & Aquarium, Tacoma WA.
- **Elsewhere in the world:**
  Australia: Great Barrier Reef Aquarium, Manly Aquarium, Melbourne Aquarium
  Canada: Vancouver Aquarium, British Columbia
  Europe: Blue Reef Aquariums, Britain; Kattegatcentret, Denmark; Fenit Sea World, Ireland; Genoa Aquarium, Italy; Musée de la Mer, Biarritz, Spain
  Japan: Osaka Aquarium, Nagoya Public Aquarium, Enoshima Aquarium
  New Zealand: PML Aquarium
  South Africa, Middle East: Cape Town's Aquarium, Durban Aquarium, Two Oceans Aquarium in South Africa; Underwater Observation Park, Eilat, Israel
  South America: Aquarium Natal, Brazil

Author & photographers

In 35 years of photographing and filming wildlife under the sea, Howard Hall has worked nose-to-nose with sharks of many species. Educated as a marine biologist, Howard soon let his underwater camera talents loose on projects like the "Wild Kingdom" episodes. Later he began to direct and produce dozens of films about sharks and other creatures of the deep for NOVA, PBS, and others. His dedication and ability to capture unusual behaviors on film have made him the recipient of six Emmys, a Golden Panda, and numerous honors.

Howard and Michele, his wife of 25 years and an Emmy-winning photographer and producer herself, now concentrate on co-producing and filming IMAX® specials and marine wildlife documentaries seen worldwide. Together and individually, the Halls also write books on marine topics from kelp forests to dolphins and produce articles and photos for magazines from *National Geographic* to *Ocean Realm*.

All the majestic photos of sharks in this book were shot by Howard and Michele Hall. Her pictures, copyrighted as Michele Hall/www.howardhall.com, appear on pp 6-7, 10-11, 17, 22, 33, 34, 43, and 47. The rest of the wildlife images are by Howard Hall. The delightful photo of Howard and Michele above was taken and is copyrighted by Peter Kragh.

▶ A sand tiger shark off the coast of North Carolina swims with half-opened mouth, showing its deadly jagged teeth.

Helping organizations and good websites

- The Halls' own website combines stirring photos and video clips with wonderful stories about underwater adventures and funny tales of Howard's misadventures with sharks and other marine life. (www.howardhall.com)
- Earthwatch Institute, 3 Clock Tower Place #100, Maynard MA 01754, links scientists, volunteers and research projects on sharks and coral reef habitats, providing solid data for conservation efforts. Kids 10 and up, teens, and families can participate in special programs, too. (www.earthwatch.org)
- This PBS television website provides a fun-filled source of info about the making of the Halls' 5-part film and companion book, "Secrets of the Ocean Realm." (www.pbs.org/oceanrealm)
- Bite-back, a UK-based activist group, works to remove shark meat and products from restaurant menus and stores worldwide; their eloquent website on threatened species tells what you can do to help. (www.bite-back.com)
- Pelagic Shark Research Foundation, 100 Shaffer Rd, Santa Cruz CA 95060. (www.pelagic.org)
- IUCN (International Union for the Conservation of Nature) promotes worldwide shark conservation. (www.iucn.org)
- International Shark Attack File. Facts and statistics about dangerous shark species and attacks at this site. (www.flmnh.ufl.edu/fish/Sharks/ISAF/ISAF.htm)
- Monterey Bay National Marine Sanctuary. This sanctuary protects 276 miles of California nearshore, home and nursery to many shark species. (www.mbnms.nos.noaa.gov)

To learn more

Books

- *Secrets of the Ocean Realm,* by Michele & Howard Hall. (Carroll & Graf/Beyond Words Publication 1997). Companion book to a television series filmed and produced by the Halls; lots of exciting behavioral photos and stories, many on sharks and rays.
- *The Kelp Forest* and *A Charm of Dolphins* by Howard Hall. Originally published in the 1990s, now scheduled to be revised and updated by London Town Press, these books present more wonderful imagery and first-person secrets from the author-photographer.
- *Sharks* by Andrea & Antonella Ferrari. (Firefly Books 2002). Useful, photo-rich guide to 120 species of sharks, rays, and chimaeras; has interviews with Howard Hall and other well-known underwater photographers.

Videos & DVDs

- "Deep Sea 3D", a 2006 IMAX® sequel to the hit "Into the Deep," is the Halls' most ambitious film yet.
- "Into the Deep." Warner Home Studio, 2004. An IMAX® DVD. 35 minutes. Directed by Howard Hall, originally released as a VHS film in 1991.
- "Coral Reef Adventure." Macgillivray Freeman Films, 2003. An IMAX® DVD; also VHS. 73 minutes. Filmed by Michele and Howard Hall, who also do on-camera narration; a global look at coral reefs and sharks in residence—and what their fates may be.
- "Island of the Sharks." NOVA/WGBH & Howard Hall Productions, 2002. An IMAX® DVD & VHS. Directed by Howard, produced by Michele, it's 75 minutes of spectacular, unusual footage at Cocos Island.
- "Underwater Trilogy." Image Entertainment, 2002. DVD. 156 minute, 3-part film by Howard Hall, exploring sharks and other hunters and hunted; alliances between marine creatures; and the demands made on animals by the aquatic life.
- "Secrets of the Ocean Realm." PBS, 1997. 5-part series, available as a set from PBS. Filmed and produced by the Halls.

Index

Photographs are numbered in **boldface** and follow the print references after **PP** (photo page).